Financial GPS: Sound Direction for Your Retirement

D. Anthony Wright

CONTENTS

INTRODUCTION

Hello! I am Anthony Wright, CEO and Senior Advisor of Retirement Specialty Group, Inc. with offices in Knoxville, Chattanooga, and our corporate office in Sparta, Tennessee. You may know me as the host of a syndicated financial radio show, "RETIRE THE WRIGHT WAY" or maybe you've seen me featured weekly as the guest expert financial advisor on the CBS affiliates in Knoxville and Chattanooga. Some of you may not know me at all. No matter what has brought you here, welcome and thank you.

In my years of practice as a financial advisor, I have seen it all when it comes to retirement planning. One common thread among everyone that I have ever spoken with is a desire for a peaceful and secure retirement. The tough reality is that not everyone accomplishes that type of retirement.

Why do some people reach a peaceful and secure retirement while others don't? You may be thinking that successful retirees simply made more money during their professional career, and making more money does in fact help. However, the one critical component of success retirement is planning. Successful retirees know it, and now you do too! **A well-designed, diligently followed plan is the key to financial retirement success.**

If you wanted to drive from Knoxville, Tennessee to Albany, New York, you would enter the destination coordinates into your GPS navigation system on your smart phone or in your car. In seconds, the clever machine would generate the best route for you to follow. It would guide you turn by turn to your destination, and even help you get back on track if you accidentally turned left instead of right.

My intention for this book is to serve as your personal Financial GPS. It will not replace advice from trusted and well-trained professionals. However, it will give you ideas that you can implement on your own, and questions to ask of specialists on your team, so that you can make the best decisions with your money.

You have worked hard to have a good life in retirement. Let's make it happen together, one turn at a time!

Regulatory Issues

This publication contains the opinions and ideas of its author.

The strategies outlined in this book may not be suitable for every individual and are not guaranteed or warranted to produce any particular results. The author is not an attorney, and does not give legal advice.

Presentations of performance data herein does not imply that similar results will be achieved in the future. Any such data are provided merely for illustrative and discussion purposes rather than focusing on the time periods used or the results derived. The reader shall focus instead on the underlying principles.

This book is sold with the understanding that neither publisher nor author through this book is engaged in rendering legal advice, tax advice, investment, insurance, financial, accounting, or any other professional advice or services. If the reader requires such advice or services, a competent professional should be consulted. Relevant laws vary from state to state.

No warranty is made with respect to the accuracy or the completeness of the information contained herein, and both the author and the publisher specifically disclaim any responsibility for any liability, loss, or risk, personal or otherwise, that is incurred as a consequence, directly or indirectly, of the use and application of any of the contents of this book.

Lastly, this book is written under the right of the First Amendment to the Constitution of the United States. This book is written as an outside business activity from my investment, advisory, and securities business. The ideas expressed are not meant to be taken as advice that you can act upon. You should find an individual advisor that you trust to implement these ideas after determining if they are appropriate and suitable for your unique situation.

Insurance products and annuities are guaranteed by the insurance companies themselves. The safety of these accounts is dependent on the claims paying ability of the insurance companies.

CHAPTER 1.
YOU NEED A RETIREMENT PLAN

You have been working hard for several decades.

Chances are you are looking forward to some rest,

relaxation, and fun in retirement. Some people want

to travel. Others just want to focus on their golf

game. No matter how you imagine your post-work

days, one thing is certain: your regular paychecks will

stop.

Once you decide to retire, you will have to rely on

other sources of income to pay for your lifestyle.

Now, everyone's lifestyle is different. Maybe you want to travel to Europe every year. Someone else might want to buy a motor home and drive across America to see every majestic state. No matter how you want to live in retirement, you are going to need a plan.

From my work, I know first-hand that most Americans are not prepared for retirement. A successful transition to retirement takes more than accumulating a certain amount of money in a pension plan or a savings account! Unless you have carefully considered your income and your expenses and mapped out your plan for sustaining your lifestyle in retirement, you are not as prepared as you think you are.

Why do so many people delay retirement planning? Here are a few myths and excuses I have heard over the years.

Myth # 1: It is too late to start.

There is no such thing as too late to start. No matter how old you are and how much you have in your bank account, there are always things you can do to improve your situation. Don't get me wrong - starting at 35 is better than starting at 50. However, with life expectancy at almost 80, it is far better to start at 50 than not start at all!

Myth # 2: It is too soon to start.

Are you kidding? The sooner you start, the better your chances are of retiring with over a million dollars in your accounts on minimal weekly contributions! When planning for retirement, remember that time is your friend, and more of it is better.

Myth # 3: I have a good amount saved, and since my cost of living in retirement will go down, I have nothing to worry about.

A lot of people believe that their cost of living in retirement will be lower than it is today. In reality, your cost of living may stay the same or even increase.

If you are a home owner, your mortgage payment will stay the same unless you pay it off. Older houses can also mean more expensive repairs. If you choose to rent, you would have to downsize considerably before you see significant savings.

Medical costs are on the rise. As you get older, chances are you'll need more tests, medications, and procedures.

Add to that the daily expenses of food, transportation, and personal care essentials that increase every year because of inflation. There is no logical reason to simply assume your overall expenses will go down simply because you no longer work.

Myth # 4: I have to pay off my debt / pay for my kids' college before I start thinking about retirement savings.

What many people don't realize is that retirement planning is not an either / or game. You can continue to pay off your debt, contribute to your kids' education, AND save for retirement. If you are in a good place financially, you are in a better position to take care of your family as opposed to becoming a burden to them.

Myth # 5: I only have to worry about my own expenses in retirement, so I'll be fine.

Life changes don't always go one way. Kids may move out to go to college, only to turn around and move back in because they cannot find a good job. Add in the possibility of supporting grandkids, or taking care of your own aging parents, and suddenly your nest egg has to stretch in ways you may not have anticipated. Your retirement savings may be covering the expenses of more people than you had originally planned.

As you can see, there are plenty of made-up ideas that people use to avoid planning for retirement. That is truly unfortunate. A good plan can help you make the most of what you have in ways that matter to you.

What makes a great retirement plan? In my experience, it is much like a recipe: a few basic ingredients and optional mix-ins to make it your own. So, let's look at some ingredients of a great retirement plan!

Ingredients of a great retirement plan

1. It is rooted in reality.

A great retirement plan is not a pie-in-the-sky grand idea. Dreaming about retirement and the things you want to enjoy in your free time is great, but building a plan with dreams alone is not realistic.

This book will walk you through the steps to ensure your plan is built on a solid foundation of facts and reality. We will consider your monthly budget, and think about your lifestyle going forward.

2. It is holistic.

A great retirement plan is holistic – which is another way of saying that it includes every possible source of income in one strategic picture. Instead of looking at Social Security benefits here and savings accounts over there, we bring everything together so that you can make informed decisions.

We also consider all possible risks. Medical care, market performance, and home ownership expenses all have a way of creeping up on you at the least convenient moment. No one can eliminate all risks – but we can be better educated, informed, and prepared.

3. It is flexible.

Dwight D. Eisenhower said, *"Plans are worthless, but planning is indispensable."* We are surrounded by continuous change, and even the best plans are outdated by the time the ink is dry.

Does that mean you should skip planning? No. It just means your plan must be revisited from time to time. People get married and divorced, grandbabies are born, health changes, and the real estate market goes up and down. Make sure your plan stays flexible.

4. It is YOURS.

The best retirement plan is YOUR retirement plan. I don't care if you bought a computer program that maps it out for you, or if you found a book by a brilliant financial guru. If the plan is not based on your circumstances and does not reflect your values, it is worthless. You won't follow it.

Here is a reality check for you. Between now and your retirement, you will watch stock markets go up and down in ways that are downright terrifying. You could get sick or run into unexpected repairs on the house. You may even need a new car. Sticking to the plan may get difficult. You need to be 100% behind your plan in order to set yourself up for success.

This may sound a little intimidating. **Based on my years of experience and hundreds of clients I have helped, I can tell you that you no matter where you are right now, you will finish this book with a better idea on how to organize your financial life in retirement.** You will learn many simple steps you can take to improve the situation. I will also teach you to spot the moments when you need to get a specialist involved.

So, let's get started with setting up your **Financial GPS!** First stop: a closer look at where you are today.

CHAPTER 2
A CLOSER LOOK AT YOUR MONEY

You might have a strict budget and know exactly how much money you have in every single account. Some of you may have no idea what your monthly income and expense numbers looks like. No matter how comfortable you are with budgeting, let's start with some basics.

The idea of a budget is really quite simple. Underneath all the complex line items, expense categories, and receipt-saving, a budget is a tool that helps you keep your expenses below your income. Money in must be greater than money out. Here is a simple picture to help you remember this.

MONEY IN > MONEY OUT

Of course, there is more to budgeting than managing your bottom line. **The point of the budgeting exercise is in matching your money with your values.** Let's say you really want to travel to Arizona twice a year to visit your grandkids. Or maybe you have a family tradition of attending the opening of the Indianapolis 500 every year. Whatever is important to you, a budget can help you make sure it happens.

Let's begin with the fun part: your income. Make a complete list of all of your money sources today. Here are some ideas.

- Paycheck from your regular job

- Money you make on the side

- Investment income (interest and dividends)

- Income from rental properties

- Alimony

- Disability payments

Now comes the more difficult part: your expenses. Pull out your bank and credit card statements for the last month (or three), and make a list of all your cash outflows. Here are some ideas on what to include.

- Mortgage or rent payment

- Utilities

- Home repairs

- Transportation expenses

- Food

- Medical expenses

- Dry-cleaning

- Loan payments

- Club memberships

- Entertainment

- Gifts

- Taxes

Next to each expense item, note whether it is essential (required for survival) or discretionary (in other words, a nice-to-have optional perk). For most people, housing expense is essential – if you don't pay your rent, you have no place to live. At the same time, country club membership might be discretionary – nice to have, but if you had to go without it, you would survive.

How did you do? If your income is greater than your expenses, that's great! I want you to use this income and expense chart to think about how your financial picture will change in retirement. Will you be able to have the things and the experiences that matter to you? If you had to cut expenses, what things would you sacrifice?

If your expenses exceed your income, don't despair. The good news is that you are done with the scariest part of the exercise. Now you have the information you need to make different decisions going forward.

Remember: knowing is always better than not knowing.

Exercises: What does money mean to you?

If listing income and expenses was a tough task for you, I encourage you to reflect on your relationship with money. Many of our beliefs about money go back to the early days. **When did you first learn the value of money?** Who taught you about it? What was the context?

I asked one of my clients, Anna, about the first time she learned the value of money. Anna grew up during the depression. Both of Anna's parents worked outside the home and struggled to make ends meet. At five years old, Anna did not fully understand the value of money and how hard her parents really did work for every dime that came into the household.

One day, Anna and her mother stopped at the local five and dime to buy a much needed pair of shoes for her brother. Anna caught sight of a beautiful porcelain china doll. She begged her mother to purchase the doll for her, but her mother explained they could not afford the $1 doll. Exasperated and in tears, Anna had a temper tantrum right in the middle of the store. Her mother, tired and worn, angrily scolded her and said, "Would you rather have that silly doll and send your brother to school barefoot?"

That is a powerful message about money for a five year old girl. The story moves Anna to tears to this day. As an adult, she understands that her parents always did the best they could for the family. The bottom line is, some of what our parents and grandparents have taught us about money maybe valuable, and other lessons may not serve us.

Another exercise you might try is to draw your money life path. The idea is to map out your life's high and low points in regards to your financial situation. Think of it as a cardiogram that illustrates your relationship with money. Were there times you may have faltered – by not earning enough, spending too much, finding yourself in a money crisis? The timeline can help you pinpoint the time when you went off-track. Here is an example to get you started.

Great Job

First Real Job

Paid Off Debt

Worked in College

Born Lower-Middle Class

Credit Card Debt Divorce

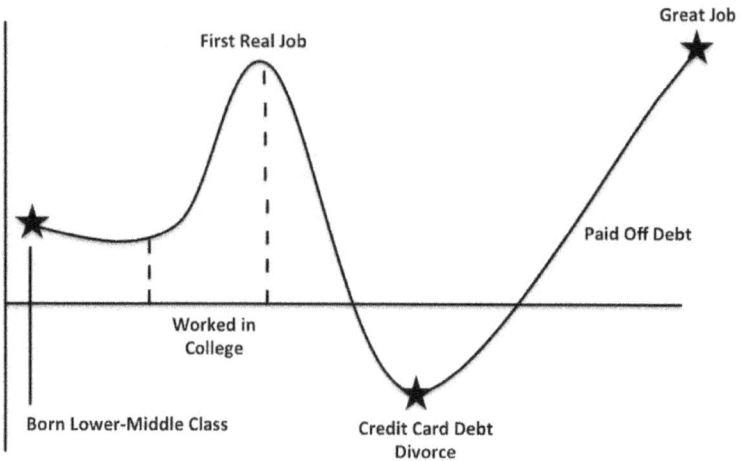

In my experience, most people have some hang-ups when it comes to money. The point of completing these exercises is to identify beliefs and attitudes that inform how you approach budgeting, retirement planning, and spending. Shining a light on your money monsters might just let you take back the wheel.

I hope that by looking at your budget and your beliefs about money, you feel more empowered to map out the rest of your journey to retirement. Our next stop: Social Security.

CHAPTER 3
MAXIMIZE YOUR SOCIAL SECURITY

Social Security benefits will form a backbone for your income stream in retirement. It makes sense to maximize them.

I always remind my clients that Social Security was originally meant to replace **a portion** of your paycheck if you could no longer work due to injury or old age. It was never meant to cover all of your needs in retirement.

As a general rule, relying on Social Security alone won't make for a stress-free retirement. That being said, you've got to get the most out of what you have. So, here is what you need to know about Social Security.

Earn more while you work

Your earnings have a direct correlation to your Social Security benefits. So there is more to a higher salary than simply bringing home a bigger paycheck right now! Consider working a second job, negotiating for a raise, or changing jobs as a strategy for boosting your annual earnings while you still can do that.

Work for more years

You must have at least of 10 years of work history in order to qualify for Social Security benefits. However, the benefit calculation takes into account your 35 best-paid years. If you only work 10 years, the zeros you earn in the other 25 years will mean a lower average payment. Working longer than 35 years can boost your benefit amount if you are earning more now than you were at the beginning of your work history.

Important dates

You can elect to receive Social Security as early as age 62. However, if you do so, your monthly benefit checks will be reduced by anywhere between 25% and 30%. The closer you get to your normal retirement age, the more earned benefit you will receive.

If you want to receive a full benefit check, you must wait until normal retirement age to apply for retirement benefits. Normal retirement age varies from 65 to 67 depending on your year of birth – here is a helpful chart with some details.

Normal Retirement Age by Birth Year

Age 62	Earliest possible age you can sign up for benefits.

Age 65	Full benefit available for people born in 1937 and earlier. Full retirement age is 65 and two months for people born in 1938, and increases by two months for every year after that until reaching 65 and ten months for people born in 1942.
Age 66	Full benefit available for people born between 1943 and 1954. Full retirement age then increases by two months for every year: from 66 and two months for those born in 1955, to 66 and ten months for those born in 1959.

Age 67	Everyone born in year 1960 or later can begin to claim full Social Security benefits at age 67.
Age 70	Social Security payments will increase by about 8% per year for every year if you delay starting the benefits until you are 70. After that point, there is no added benefit to delaying the benefits.

What if you are disabled and cannot work until your full retirement age? Consider filing for disability payments first. The check will be larger than your reduced retirement benefit, and once you reach your normal retirement age the disability payments will convert to retirement payments.

Consider your family situation

Married couples have options when it comes to claiming benefits. Each spouse can choose to receive the benefits based on his own earnings history, or opt into getting up to 50% of what the higher earning spouse is eligible for. Coordinate payments with your spouse for maximum benefit.

If you are widowed, you can apply for Social Security survivor benefits when you are 60 years old (or 50 years old if you are disabled). Generally, you must have been married for at least 9 months to qualify for survivor benefits; however, there are exceptions to the rule.

Divorce is an important consideration. If you were married for at least 10 years, you are treated as a spouse for the purposes of Social Security benefits, provided you do not remarry. Your ex-spouse and you must both be at least 62 years old for you to receive benefits.

Social Security taxes

Your Social Security benefits may be subject to tax. This can happen if your other income sources (continued paycheck, rental income, or investment income) push you over what is called the base line.

Here is how it works. Add up all your taxable income, tax-free income, and one half of your Social Security benefits. If the amount is over $25,000 for a single filer or $32,000 for a married couple filing jointly, your Social Security benefits can be taxable. If you are married and filing separately, you may have to pay tax on your Social Security benefits.

Looking ahead

The state of the Social Security fund continues to raise concern. The latest reports projects that the program will have enough resources to continue with payments as scheduled until 2034. After that, the Social Security fund will only have enough money to pay out about 79% of benefits.

The government could choose a variety of ways to deal with that fund shortage. Some options include increasing normal retirement age, changing how the inflation adjustment to benefits is calculated, cutting the benefits, or a combination of all three.

When my clients bring up their concerns about the state of Social Security, I recommend that they stay informed and focus on the things that they can personally influence and change. It does not serve you to lose sleep over the Social Security funding shortfall – there is nothing you can do about it anyway. It is much better to put your focus where it will make a difference. Your own savings and investing strategies are great places to start – we will address them in CHAPTER 5.

Now, on to the Social Security companion: Medicare.

CHAPTER 4
WHAT YOU NEED TO KNOW ABOUT MEDICARE

Almost all working Americans pay into the Medicare system. While signing up for Medicare is a significant milestone and a relief for many people, the program comes with enough complexities and stipulations to make your head spin.

Here are the basics you need to know.

- **Medicare Part A** covers hospital stays, hospice care, and certain home care expenses.

- **Medicare Part B** pays for doctors' visits, labs, outpatient care, physical therapy, and certain preventative care.

- **Medicare Part C** is essentially Medicare Parts A, B, and D delivered through Medicare-approved private companies. There are usually restrictions on coverage.

- **Medicare Part D** is for prescription drug coverage.

Once you decide whether the combination of Medicare Parts A, B, and D (public route) or Medicare Part C (private route) is right for you, here are your next considerations.

1. Sign up on time

Most people are eligible to sign up for Medicare Part A and Part B three months before they turn 65. Don't wait! Signing up later can delay the start of your coverage, and may even result in late enrollment penalties.

If you are already receiving Social Security benefits, your Medicare benefits will be triggered automatically – just look for the Medicare card in the mail.

2. Plan for costs

Just like a private insurance plan, Medicare has co-pays, deductibles, and coinsurance. Your out of pocket costs could be significant, and having a financial reserve in the event of high healthcare expenses can make a difference.

3. Look into supplemental plans

Supplementing your Medicare coverage with another insurance plan can be an effective way to control healthcare costs. Medigap policies are sold by private insurance companies. They cover copayments, coinsurance, and deductibles. They can even cover certain expenses that Medicare won't cover.

The best time to get your Medigap policy is during the six months after you turn 65 and enroll in Medicare Part B. Once your enrollment period begins, it cannot be delayed or paused – so don't wait! After your six months are up, getting a

Medigap policy becomes more expensive and in some cases impossible.

4. Remember prescription drug coverage

Let's face it – medication is expensive. As you get older, there is a good chance you may need more of it. My best advice is to shop around for the best-fit prescription drug coverage plan for you. The not-so-fun part of this exercise is that if you want to continue getting the best value policy, you will have to re-assess your options every year.

Here are a few more tips on choosing the right plan.

- Remember that lower premiums can mean higher deductibles, so analyze your needs to buy the right amount of coverage for the year.

- Every year, make sure the drugs that are vital for you right now (or are likely to become vital in the upcoming year) are still covered under your new policy.

- A plan could have specific rules about where you can fill your prescription. Be sure that there is a convenient pick-up location near you.

- Some plans require that you try a lower-cost generic version of a medication before you can get approval for a more expensive one.

The bottom line is, do your research. Sometimes paying a little more to get less hassle is a fair exchange!

5. Protect your Medicare ID the same way you protect your Social Security number.

This should go without saying, but you must protect your Medicare number the same way you protect the rest of your personal identity. You would not give out your Social Security number to someone who called your house (at least I hope not!) – so don't do it with your Medicare number!

Medicare fraud is real, and thousands of dollars are wasted every year on unnecessary and unauthorized equipment, tests, and medications. Check your statements every month, and if you spot something unusual, call your doctor.

Now that we have covered the basics of Social Security and Medicare, our GPS is pointing to the next stop: savings accounts and investments. No matter what your comfort level is with investments, the reality is that your interest and dividend must at least cover inflation! You don't have to figure out investing on your own, but there are definite steps you can take to find yourself in a better place.

CHAPTER 5
GET THE MOST OUT OF YOUR SAVINGS

If you are like most of my clients, you have worked

hard your entire life and saved what you could

towards your retirement. Those savings might be in

a bank account, in a 401(k), or in an IRA. Regardless

of where your money lives right now, this is the time

to get a piece of paper and make a complete list of

all your accounts. While you do that, let's go over

some basics.

- Bank accounts will include your checking and savings accounts. It is helpful to write down how much interest each account is earning.

- List all of the relevant Certificates of Deposit (CDs) with their expiration dates, as well.

- Your 401(k) accounts are essentially retirement savings accounts that are invested in mutual funds, stocks, or bonds. Your employer may or may not have contributed to them. You can generally take your own contributions with you when you change jobs. The employer match "vests" after you have worked at a company for a number of years.

- An IRA (Individual Retirement Account) is an account that you can contribute to for yourself and for your family members. It is

usually invested similar to a 401(k) account.
The maximum annual contribution amount
for an IRA is lower than for a 401(k) plan, but
IRAs make a good supplement to a 401(k)
plan.

Now that we have covered the basics, here is what
you need to do in order to get the most out of the
money you have saved.

Manage your risk

Here is a fact for you: any account that is not FDIC-
insured can lose money. So, if you keep your money
anywhere outside a bank account, there is a
possibility you may lose some or even all of it.
Certain investments are riskier than others: generally

speaking, a US Treasury bond is less risky than a stock in a biotechnology start-up company.

Risk and market fluctuations can be scary, especially if your retirement date is near. I tell my clients that they must understand the risks they are taking with money. It is generally wise to decrease the amount of accepted risk as you get older.

I will explain with a simple example. Let's say your 22-year old daughter just got her first corporate job. She is lucky enough to have an employer-matched 401(k) plan, and smart enough to begin contributing to it right away. Her 401(k) account is probably invested in a mix of mutual funds, stocks, and bonds.

With the market today going up and down like a rollercoaster, it is possible that her account balance will increase and drop considerably at times over the next few years. That rollercoaster does not really matter to her, because she won't need to touch her 401(k) money for the next 40 years. Over her working life, the investments will likely earn more interest and dividends than a bank account would. Because your daughter is so young, she can simply wait out the market insanity and benefit from the good years in the market.

The situation is completely different for someone close to retirement. A smart guy by the name of A. Gary Shilling once said, *"Markets can remain irrational a lot longer than you and I can remain solvent."* In other words, your expenses may force you to take money out of the investment accounts at the bottom of the market – which is not a happy place to be.

Lesson learned? As you get closer to retirement, give good thought to how much risk you are willing to take on.

Simplify

Simplifying your investment accounts is good advice for people of any age. You are a pretty smart person, so here is what I want for you to keep in mind. Any time you encounter an investment or an account that you cannot understand and explain in simple terms, think twice before you sign anything. Sure, there are some complex financial terms and concepts out there. **However, at the most basic level you should be able to understand where your money is, why it is there, and what it is doing for you.**

Here is an example from a name you will recognize. Warren Buffett, a multimillionaire investor, is known to have a basket in his office marked "Too hard". Now, the guy is brilliant. Hundreds of investors try to copy his strategy. Buffett's guiding philosophy is that if something seems too hard to figure out, it is not worth his time or effort. Good ideas are simple.

A few of you may be thinking about picking your own investments. Do you know what each company you consider does? Is it better than its competition? Do you use that company's product or services? Do you trust its management with your money? In other words, have you done your research?

And by research, I don't mean watching the 5 o'clock news. In fact, here is a picture for you from Carl Richards, a financial planner and a New York

Times columnist who can explain virtually anything

on the back of a cocktail napkin.

BAD IDEA!

Choose your sources wisely. Remember that

investing is a job, and if you are going to take risks

with your hard-earned money, you had better put

time and energy into thinking it through.

Choose your advisor wisely

If making your own investment decisions is in your personal "Too hard" basket, that's OK too. In my opinion, it is far better to delegate this task to someone who is trained and trusted than to give it an occasional half-hearted effort on your own.

There are several things to consider when choosing an investment or financial advisor. First of all, there are nearly 300,000 financial advisors in the United States. That's a lot of advisors across the country, and dozens of them are probably in your own neighborhood. How are you supposed to choose?

Well, I cannot tell you who you should pick. What I can do is tell you what I would do if I were in your shoes.

First of all, check certifications. Many advisors have a veritable alphabet soup after their last names! Research the abbreviations and ask the advisor about his certificates and what they mean.

Once that is out of the way, consider these additional ideas to guide your search.

- **Referrals are always a good place to start.** Ask your friends and family about the financial advisors they are using, especially if they are happy with their choice.

- **Ask the advisor how he gets paid.** Some advisors charge a flat fee for the services they provide, others get a commission based on the amount of money they manage, yet others charge hourly. Depending on your needs, different fee structures might work best – that is why it is a good idea to talk to more than one advisor.

- **Ask him about his investment philosophy.** You are looking for someone who can be prudent on your behalf, and won't talk you into anything overly risky.

- **Pick an advisor who can approach your financial situation holistically.** That means considering all of your income sources, expenses, and taxes. You are a whole person, so it does not make sense to only look at one account at a time when it comes to creating your financial picture.

- **Ask the advisor about his own investments.** Depending on your advisor's age, his investment mix will look very different from yours. However, you will get a sense for whether he takes his own advice. I am a believer that financial advisors need to get their own money house in order before they can help others.

- **Get a feel for the office.** Is the advisor's assistant polite, professional, and patient? Are they pleasant on the phone when you call, or do you feel like a nuisance every time you ask a question?

- **Choose the advisor who connects with you as a person.** If you are getting a feeling that the advisor is not really listening to you, consider looking at your other options.

Lastly, consider bringing your spouse with you as you interview financial advisors. Chances are, one of you will outlive the other – and it helps to hire an advisor who will be there for both of you.

Your financial advisor, if you decide to work with one, will be your personal guide on the road to retirement and beyond. This person will help you draw the map, plan the route, and hold your hand while you walk it. He is a big part of your **Financial GPS**, so choose wisely.

CHAPTER 6
MANAGE YOUR EXPENSES IN RETIREMENT

No matter how well you think through your income sources in retirement, income is only half of the overall financial picture. You must consider your expenses if you are to have any hope of a peaceful retirement with minimal surprises.

We have already touched upon your expenses in CHAPTER 2 when the **Financial GPS** guided you through a closer look at your budget.

If you have completed the exercises, you already have a monthly budget that details how much you spend on your housing, medical bills, utilities, entertainment, and food. You also know which expenses are non-negotiable (rent or mortgage) and which ones are discretionary (country club membership).

If you have not worked through your budget, do yourself a favor – go back to CHAPTER 2 and get it done now. Advanced strategies for managing expenses won't make any sense to you if you don't have your arms around the basics.

If you have done the homework already, great job! Let's look at several advanced strategies. Some of these can take time to align just right, and not all will be right for you. However, this is a great next step if you want to make sure your nest egg outlasts you and your spouse.

Control housing costs

Let's face it – if you are like most Americans, housing is your biggest money drain. Even if you have the good fortune of owning your home, repairs on older properties can add up to several months' worth of mortgage payments due on short notice.

What are your options in retirement? Here is a list to consider.

Pay off your mortgage

Consider paying off your mortgage faster. A good chunk of your mortgage payment is going towards interest, not the principle of the loan. If your cash flow allows it, pay off the mortgage by making extra payments and putting your tax refunds towards the balance.

Remember insurance

Carry appropriate insurance on the home that will cover a disaster scenario (fire, hurricane) as well as more routine repairs. Shop around for policies to be sure that you are getting the optimal amount of coverage at the best rate.

When choosing an insurance policy, pay attention to how the insurance company calculates the amount you will receive in the event of a loss. Replacement value is a payment based on what it would cost you today to replace what you have lost. Actual cash value is equal to the replacement cost minus depreciation. As a policyholder, you want to get full replacement value. Insurance companies usually want to give you actual cash value because it is lower. Review the terms carefully to avoid surprises.

Consider downsizing

This can be emotionally difficult for the people who have their hearts set on retiring in the same home where they have raised the family. However, it is worth thinking through. A smaller home comes with many benefits, including a smaller mortgage payment, lower property taxes, and lower utility bills. A sale of your current home could also allow you to put a portion of sale proceeds towards retirement savings.

Think about moving to another area

You don't have to worry about your work commute or your kids' school any more. Why not think about moving someplace that will give you a comfortable climate, good medical care, and a more affordable cost of living? You don't have to move across the country to cut your living expenses – costs of living can be dramatically lower in a neighboring county or town.

For the most adventurous retirees, moving abroad may be an option. Many countries offer a lower cost of living, helping your retirement savings last longer.

If you are thinking about picking an exotic destination for retirement, gather all your facts. Quality of healthcare, transportation, and public services must all be considered carefully. A place with a vibrant expat community could be a good fit, since you would be leaving your own social circle behind. Look for a place with a stable government and economy. Think about your readiness to learn a foreign language. Add in travel costs if you plan to fly to the US regularly for family visits.

When thinking about moving for your retirement, remember to stay away from these potential problems.

- **High crime areas.** Always check crime statistics for any neighborhood you are considering. Lower cost of housing is not worth getting mugged or murdered.

- **Areas where life is uncomfortable without a car.** Chances are you will eventually have to stop driving. Choose a community with reliable public transportation and well-developed low-cost taxi and van service.

- **Areas with poorly developed infrastructure.** Well-maintained streets, public utilities, libraries, and community centers may cost a little more, but they contribute immensely to your quality of life in retirement.

Consider renting

Some retirees decide that home ownership is no longer right for them. As a renter, you don't have to pay property taxes or cover repair expenses. You also don't have to deal with many hassles of home ownership, such as shoveling snow or landscaping.

Remember to weigh those benefits against the possibility of rent increases, as well as the fact that your rent agreement is only renewed if it pleases the landlord.

On the flip side, you may decide that you want to become a landlord! Housemates can help you share the cost of housing, and bring along some welcome companionship.

Minimize taxes

Eliminating taxes altogether may or may not happen for you, but there are things you can do to minimize them.

First off, get educated on which cash flows generate tax expenses. For example, withdrawals from your

Roth IRA are not subject to taxes. Income from your side jobs, rent payments, and investments can push you into taxable territory. When in doubt, work with a trusted CPA who can help you make good decisions.

Control medical costs

Medical insurance is a good way to control your healthcare expenses. Avoid gaps in your coverage by applying for health insurance in a timely manner. As we have covered in CHAPTER 4, shop around for prescription drug coverage policies, and spend some time reading your policy. No one likes surprises!

Long term care policies can be an option for controlling the costs of care at a specialized facility or in your home. They can also be expensive.

Because this is a big topic, we leave it until

CHAPTER 7. There, we will consider your next

Financial GPS stop – various risks and ways to

address them.

CHAPTER 7
FACE THE RISKS

Let's face it – life is risky. No matter how careful we are, we can never eliminate every single possible risk. However, we can build a safety net so that risks become less devastating. Long term care insurance is a good place to start this conversation.

Long term care insurance

Many retirees purchase a long term care policy because they are scared of rising costs of care in nursing homes, assisted living facilities, and in their own homes. Peace of mind does not come cheap, as premiums can be very costly.

When looking at your potential need for care, remember that your Social Security benefits will cover a portion of the cost. Look at the statistics for average cost of care, as well as the average length of time care is needed.

Keep in mind that many long term care policies are "use it or lose it". In other words, if you have paid into a standard long term care policy for 10 years just to pass away peacefully in your sleep, you won't get any financial benefit from your coverage.

Some newer policies are hybrids between long term care and life insurance. They are structured to help pay for long term care expenses and to provide you with an income source in older years. Premiums on those hybrid policies vary dramatically, and their features and restrictions are enough to make anyone's head spin. While a hybrid policy can be a good choice for some people, you must have a solid understanding of benefits, limitations, and costs before you sign anything.

My bottom line advice is, don't buy a long term insurance policy just because you are scared! Talk to a trusted advisor who can help you sort through your options. Long term care policies can work, but you must choose carefully.

Powers of Attorney

A power of attorney is another way of describing you appointing another person or organization to make decisions for you and act on your behalf while you are unavailable or unable to do it for yourself.

There are three broad types of powers of attorney.

- **Special powers of attorney are limited to a specific act.** Perhaps you want someone else to complete the purchase of your dream car on your behalf while you are away on vacation. Another example is if you want your spouse to make medical decisions on your behalf in the event that you are unable to do it for yourself.

- **General powers of attorney cover all personal and business decisions.** Your agent is empowered to make medical decisions, business decisions, and financial decisions as if you were making them for yourself.

- **Temporary powers of attorney are time-limited.**

- **Springing (or conditional) powers of attorney only take effect in the event you are incapacitated.**

As you can see, there are circumstances when you may want to appoint someone to act on your behalf – either temporarily or until you pass on. It is smart to think through this decision before an emergency.

So, how do you choose the person to appoint as your agent?

- **Choose someone who is available.** Depending on the powers of attorney you want to assign, your agent may be taking on serious, time consuming, and emotionally challenging responsibilities and duties.

- **Be sure that your agent is capable of making good decisions.** Picking someone whose judgment you trust is critical for success. Remember: your agent's decisions will have the same weight as if you were making them yourself.

- **Consider whether the person is capable of prudent money management.** Look at how he is managing his own financial situation, and how diligent he is with legal matters.

- **Be certain that your agent understands you and shares your values.** In a medical emergency, your agent may have to decide whether or not to continue with life support.

He or she may have to choose the facility for

your care. Make your wishes known to your

agent, and be sure that he or she will carry

them out.

Depending on circumstances, you may want to appoint an

alternative agent in the event your first agent passes on.

Imagine a situation where you appoint your spouse as your

only agent to make medical decisions on your behalf. What

happens if the two of you are in a car crash that leaves your

spouse dead and you incapacitated?

Death and serious illness are difficult subjects to

consider. Most people are uncomfortable talking

about them, and will avoid this conversation for as

long as they possibly can. That is unfortunate.

It is true that this is not a fun topic. However, I urge you to consider it anyway. If you do nothing to address the financial and emotional reality of illness and death, you are leaving all those difficult decisions to your grieving family. Is that the legacy you want to leave?

Since we are on the subject of legacy, let me ask you another question. You have worked hard to follow the **Financial GPS**, figure out your budget, make the most out of your savings, and manage your expenses. Presumably, you will be leaving behind property and money after you pass on. What is the purpose of those assets?

That's precisely the topic of our next stop.

CHAPTER 8
THE PURPOSE OF MONEY

You have worked hard and planned carefully to have money and assets in retirement. Some of that money is intended to ensure that you have the resources to support yourself in retirement. Financial independence, or having a reliable flow of money to pay your living expenses, is great – but for most people it's not the final goal.

That brings us to the next **Financial GPS** stop – the question of legacy.

Your legacy

At the end of the day, after your own bills are paid, what is your money intended for? What does it mean to you to leave it behind, and how do you want to see it put to use?

This can be a tough question for many readers. Your life in this body is finite – how do you want to be remembered?

Some of my clients look at it through the frame of imagining their funeral – who comes to pay their last respects? What do people say about you?

Others think of it more like a Lifetime Achievement Award. If you were to get one of those, what would it be for? What would you say in your acceptance speech?

No matter how you approach it, give some thought to the purpose of your money. Do you intend it to be used for your grandchildren's college education? Would you like to see the money go to your favorite charity? Who would benefit from it the most? Who deserves it? Your answers will guide you to the next document that I want you to consider: your will.

You need a will

Most people avoid putting together a will the same way they avoid retirement planning. When it comes to death, people choose to think they have plenty of time until their backs are against the wall.

The reality is that not one of us knows how much time we have left. You may have another 40 healthy years ahead of you – or you may get hit by a bus next week. If an accident or serious illness happens before you have had the opportunity to document your final wishes, you have no assurance whatsoever that the money will get split the way you would approve of.

So, you have two options. You can wait and hope for the best, or you can be proactive and write a will.

If you are that rare person who has a will, keep in mind that it's a good idea to revisit the document every few years. Life brings about change. People get married and divorced. Someone mentioned in your will may have passed on, or you may have new grandchildren to account for. Your financial situation may have changed enough to demand a fresh look at the asset distribution.

Just as with the powers of attorney, give careful consideration to who you appoint as your estate executor. Distributing an estate takes attention to detail, familiarity with legal documents, business savvy, and the ability to remain calm in a stressful situation. My clients often point to their spouse or best friend as someone they would trust with the job. However, keep in mind that you must select the person who is best qualified – not necessarily one you like best.

Let's consider trusts

Trusts are legal arrangements that are created to hold property or money on behalf of an individual.

Do you need a trust? It depends. Here are a few signs that you may benefit from speaking to a professional advisor about trusts.

- You want to avoid probate.

- You want to minimize taxes.

- You want for a certain portion of your estate to be used for a specific purpose. An example would be setting up a trust to hold the money for your grandson's college tuition.

- You want for a third party to hold your assets in the event you become incapacitated and unable to manage them for yourself.

There are several basic types of trusts.

- A **living trust** is effective while you are alive.

- A **testamentary trust** becomes effective when you pass on. Testamentary trusts are usually created within wills.

- A **revocable trust** allows you to change your mind.

- An **irrevocable trust** cannot be reversed. An irrevocable trust can be a good way of protecting your assets from the reach of a nursing home. Remember that an irrevocable trust has a five year look-back window. It means that if you want to protect certain assets such as your bank accounts or your home, you must place them in in irrevocable trust five years before anything happens to you.

The one thing you need to know about trusts is that they are very complex. Sure, you could get a trust created online for as little as $300, while a consultation with a lawyer would run you $1,000-$3,000. Consider what is at stake, and remember that a mistake on trust documents can render them useless. Sometimes, peace of mind is worth paying for.

CHAPTER 9
LIFE AFTER RETIREMENT

With all the heavy financial topics behind us, the **Financial GPS** is pointing to the final destination on our path – life after retirement.

Some people have a traditional idea of what retirement is like: perhaps it involves playing golf, traveling, gardening, or just relaxing on the couch. Others want to use this newfound time and space to pursue interests they could not have focused on earlier in life. Perhaps you have always wanted to try oil painting, baking, or teaching – now is your chance!

No matter what path speaks to you right now, here are a few things I want for you to keep in mind.

1. Stay physically active.

We all get to retirement in different physical conditions. Some retirees run marathons and teach yoga, others are wheelchair-bound. No matter where you are today, do your very best to stay physically active. Many gyms offer group classes for retirees – a great opportunity to exercise and meet new people. If you would rather be outdoors, consider walking or biking regularly to keep your body moving. The power and positive impact of natural movement is critical for well-being.

2. Pay attention to your nutrition.

No, you don't have to turn to eating all-organic foods or become a vegetarian. However, I encourage you to pay attention to what you eat. Choose naturally occurring and minimally processed foods as much as you can. You don't need elaborate five-course meals to be healthy – simple ingredients, simply prepared, will keep you energized.

3. Keep your mind active.

Whether you choose to take classes at a local community college or solve crossword puzzles, remember that mental stimulation is a source of energy. Many colleges and universities allow retirees to audit classes at no charge – as long as you don't care about getting the credit, you can experience all kinds of new subjects for free. Exposure to new ideas keeps your mind sharp, and fresh faces are a good reason to get out of bed in the morning.

4. Find your purpose.

Viktor Frankl, an Austrian psychiatrist and Holocaust survivor, observed that humans can live through unimaginable hardship if they can find a meaning in it. In retirement, just as in your working life, some days will be harder than others. Knowing your reason to wake up every morning can be a great motivator when your spirits flag and your body hurts. Find your purpose, and live it.

5. Stay connected to your community.

A few years ago, National Geographic wanted to learn why people in certain parts of the world lived to be over a hundred years old while maintaining excellent quality of life. Through their research, they have found five geographic areas they named "Blue Zones" – places where more people live longer and happier lives than in the rest of the world.

One of the lessons from the Blue Zones is the importance of social connection. Healthy and happy centenarians choose personal tribes that support healthy behaviors and care about them. Whether you remain active in your church, join a volunteering group, or meet your friends every week for a game of bridge, stay connected to your community.

So, keep yourself physically and mentally active, live your purpose, and stay connected to your people.

And above all, remember that your retirement is about you – use it to do what makes you happy.

IN CLOSING
PROFESSIONS YOU NEED ON YOUR TEAM

Great job on following the **Financial GPS** to arrive at the destination – your peaceful and fulfilling retirement!

As you have followed the journey through this book, you have learned that there are many things you can do for yourself to transition to a secure retirement and leave behind a legacy that matters. You can create a budget, be smart about your Social Security, make good decisions regarding insurance, and manage your expenses.

There are also planning areas that would benefit from specialist attention. From managing investments to creating a will, some things are better left to trained professionals. Here is a short list of specialists that I think every retirement-planning client should have in the Rolodex.

- **An investment advisor or financial planner** for putting together a complete financial plan for your retirement and managing your money.

- **An attorney** for wills and trusts.

- **A CPA or an accountant** for tax planning and filing.

It is best to choose professionals that are convenient for you to visit. Be sure they are willing and able to work together for your benefit. Pick professionals who listen well, explain things patiently, and respect your risk preferences. If you are working with someone you would not recommend to a friend, it may be time to switch.

As we say goodbye, I encourage you to reflect upon your personal takeaways from this book. What was most useful? What will you do today? What was most challenging?

If you can think of someone who would benefit from reading this book, consider letting him or her borrow this copy (or better yet, recommend it or buy it for them as a gift). A book is still the cheapest way to acquire knowledge, and you might save a friend or a family member thousands of dollars and much heartache.